CONTENTS

WHO'S WHO

 Alexander the Great (356–323 B.C.) King of Macedonia and brilliant military leader. Conquered the Ancient World's largest empire.

 Philip II (c. 382–336 B.C.) King of Macedonia and Alexander's father. During his reign, Macedonia became the world's leading military power. He was assassinated by Pausanius at his daughter, Cleopatra's, wedding.

 Olympias (c. 375–316 B.C.) Wife of King Philip II and mother of Alexander and his sister Cleopatra. She was suspected of plotting to kill Philip.

Darius III (reign 336–330 B.C.) The last king of the Persian Empire and Alexander's archenemy. He was defeated several times by Alexander in battle.

 Roxane (c. 343–310 B.C.) Persian princess who married Alexander in 327 B.C. After Alexander's death, she gave birth to a son, who was also named Alexander.

 Hephaestion (c. 357–324 B.C.) Macedonian nobleman, brought up in Philip's court. Alexander's closest friend and a commander in his army. He died of a fever in Babylon.

ALEXANDER'S EMPIRE

*I*n 336 B.C., Alexander III became king of Macedonia after the murder of his father, Philip. He was 20 years old. An even more brilliant leader and soldier than his father, it took Alexander just 11 years to conquer the largest empire the Ancient World had ever known.

GREAT ALEXANDER
Alexander's conquests earned him the title of Alexander the Great.

"THIS LAND IS MINE!"
At its height, Alexander's vast empire stretched from Greece in the west to India in the east. It covered large parts of what is now Turkey, Egypt, Iran, and Afghanistan.

THE EMPIRE AT ITS HEIGHT

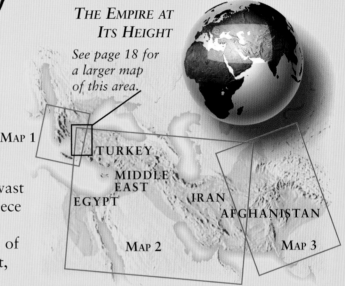

See page 18 for a larger map of this area.

MAP 1

TURKEY

MIDDLE EAST

EGYPT

IRAN

AFGHANISTAN

MAP 2

MAP 3

THE CITY STATES
Ancient Greece was divided into small, independent city states. Among them were Athens, Thebes, and Sparta. Macedonia lay to the northeast. In 338 B.C., King Philip defeated the city states and gained control of Greece. A year later, he united the Greeks and Macedonians in a common aim by declaring war on their enemy, Persia.

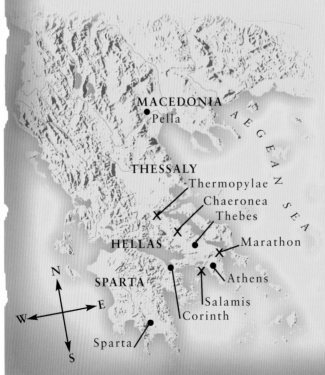

MACEDONIA
Pella
THESSALY
Thermopylae
Chaeronea
Thebes
HELLAS
Marathon
SPARTA
Athens
Salamis
Corinth
Sparta
AEGEAN SEA

N
W — E
S

MAP 1: GREECE 336 B.C. Macedonia and the Greek city states. Crosses show key battle sites.

4

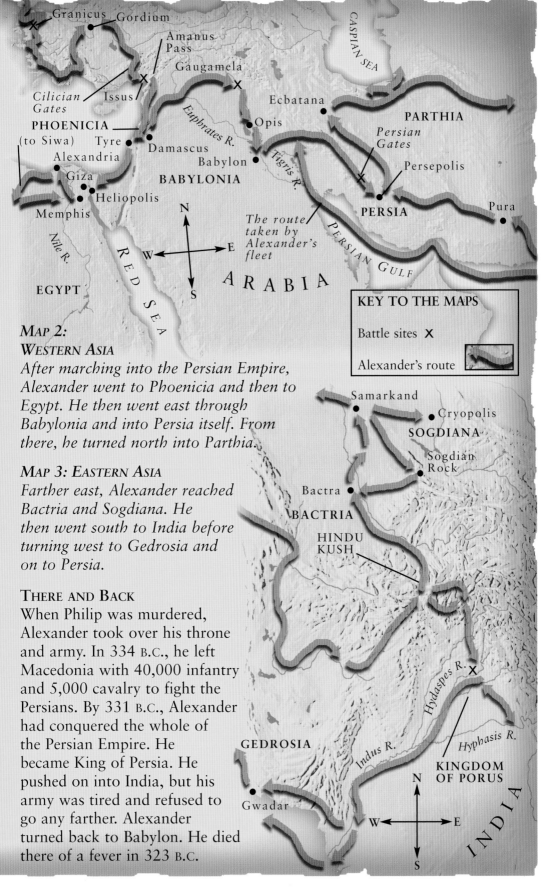

Granicus Gordium

Amanus
Pass

Gaugamela

CASPIAN SEA

Cilician
Gates
Issus

Ecbatana

PARTHIA

Persian
Gates

PHOENICIA

(to Siwa) Tyre
Alexandria
Giza
Heliopolis
Memphis

Damascus
Babylon

BABYLONIA

Euphrates R.

Opis

Tigris R.

Persepolis

PERSIA

Pura

N

W — E

S

The route
taken by
Alexander's
fleet

A R A B I A

PERSIAN GULF

Nile R.

R E D   S E A

EGYPT

KEY TO THE MAPS

Battle sites **X**

Alexander's route

MAP 2:
WESTERN ASIA
After marching into the Persian Empire,
Alexander went to Phoenicia and then to
Egypt. He then went east through
Babylonia and into Persia itself. From
there, he turned north into Parthia.

MAP 3: EASTERN ASIA
Farther east, Alexander reached
Bactria and Sogdiana. He
then went south to India before
turning west to Gedrosia and
on to Persia.

THERE AND BACK
When Philip was murdered,
Alexander took over his throne
and army. In 334 B.C., he left
Macedonia with 40,000 infantry
and 5,000 cavalry to fight the
Persians. By 331 B.C., Alexander
had conquered the whole of
the Persian Empire. He
became King of Persia. He
pushed on into India, but his
army was tired and refused to
go any farther. Alexander
turned back to Babylon. He died
there of a fever in 323 B.C.

Samarkand

Cryopolis

SOGDIANA

Sogdian
Rock

Bactra

BACTRIA

HINDU
KUSH

Hydaspes R.

Hyphasis R.

GEDROSIA

Indus R.

KINGDOM
OF PORUS

N

W — E

S

Gwadar

INDIA

5

ALEXANDER'S WORLD

In Alexander's day, many different peoples fought for power in the Ancient World. Alexander took full advantage of the situation to expand his vast empire.

THE MACEDONIANS

The kingdom of Macedonia lay to the northeast of Greece. (Today, Macedonia is part of Greece.) The Macedonians claimed to be descended from Macedon, the son of Zeus. They thought of themselves as Greeks, but many Greeks did not. The Greeks saw Macedonia as poor and backward. In the fifth and sixth centuries B.C., Macedonia was invaded many times and split by civil war. But when Philip II came to the throne in 359 B.C. this changed. Over the next 23 years, Philip set out to unite the country and expand its territory. A brilliant soldier and organizer, Philip made Macedonia the greatest power in the region. When he was murdered in 336 B.C., his son Alexander took control.

A small carving believed to be of Alexander's father, Philip of Macedonia.

GODS AND SUPERSTITIONS
The Ancient Greeks and Macedonians believed in many gods and goddesses. The most important were the 12 Olympians, ruled by Zeus. Before any important project, people tried to learn the will of the gods. They might ask a priest to read the omens, or consult an oracle. An oracle was a shrine where a priest or priestess spoke on behalf of the gods.

The goddess Athene

THE GREEKS

Philip and Alexander took advantage of fighting between the Greek city states to expand their empire. During the fifth century B.C., Greece took part in two great wars. In the Persian Wars (490–449 B.C.), the city states joined forces to defeat the Persians, but Greece's new unity did not last long. The Peloponnesian War (431–404 B.C.) between Athens and Sparta lasted for 27 years and split the country. In the squabbling that followed, Macedonia made its move. At the Battle of Chaeronea in 338 B.C., Philip defeated the city states and took control of Greece.

ALEXANDER'S ARMY

Alexander inherited a tough, well-trained army from his father. It was divided into cavalry and infantry, made up of foot soldiers, javelin men, and archers. In battle, Alexander often used the tactics shown on the right. The cavalry attacked the right end of the enemy infantry, causing a gap to open in the lines. Then the infantry moved in from behind to finish off the attack.

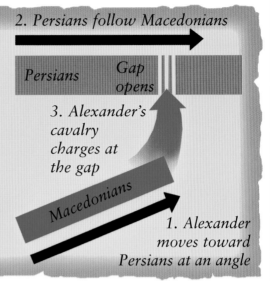

2. Persians follow Macedonians

Persians Gap opens

3. Alexander's cavalry charges at the gap

Macedonians

1. Alexander moves toward Persians at an angle

THE PERSIANS

The Persians came from the area now called Iran. During the sixth century B.C., they began to expand their territory and soon conquered a huge empire. In 546 B.C., the Persians seized the Greek colonies on the west coast of Asia. In 490 B.C., they invaded Greece and began the Persian Wars. Although a peace treaty was signed, most Greeks continued to hate and fear the Persians. Putting their problems aside, the Greeks joined the Macedonians against their common enemy – the Persians.

THE EGYPTIANS

In 525 B.C., Egypt became part of the Persian Empire. But the Persians were unpopular rulers who showed no respect for Egyptian religion and culture. Rebellions soon broke out and, in 404 B.C., Egypt won independence. In 343 B.C., however, the Persians took back Egypt. Alexander then arrived in 332 B.C. and captured Egypt from the Persians. Shortly afterward, Alexander was made pharaoh, or king, of Egypt.

A Roman mosaic showing King Darius of Persia at the Battle of Issus.

ALEXANDER the GREAT
THE LIFE OF A KING AND CONQUEROR

AH, PRINCE ALEXANDER! WHAT DO YOU HAVE TO SHOW THE CLASS? I HOPE IT IS **BETTER** THAN THE LITTLE FLIES AND WORMS YOUR FRIENDS HAVE MANAGED TO FIND.

ARISTOTLE! LOOK, TEACHER!

11

AUGUST 338 B.C. ALEXANDER IS NOW 18 AND HAS **GROWN** ENOUGH TO BECOME AN OFFICER IN PHILIP'S CAVALRY. HE IS ABOUT TO **FIGHT** HIS FIRST BATTLE.

AS EXPECTED, THE CITY STATES PATCH UP THEIR DIFFERENCES AND **DECLARE WAR** ON PHILIP.* THE TWO ARMIES MEET AT CHAERONEA.

*SEE PAGE 4 FOR CITY STATES.

PHILIP'S INFANTRY IS ON THE **RIGHT** SIDE OF THEIR ARMY. ALEXANDER AND THE CAVALRY ARE ON THE **LEFT**. PHILIP'S PHALANX ATTACKS FIRST.

GET **READY** TO GIVE THE SIGNAL.

THE MACEDONIANS RETREAT WITH THE ATHENIANS CLOSE ON THEIR HEELS.

THERE'S THE GAP!

THE CHARGING ATHENIANS LEAVE A GAP IN THE GREEK LINE. ALEXANDER BREAKS THROUGH IT AND CIRCLES THE GREEKS, WHO PANIC. THOSE WHO DO NOT RUN ARE **KILLED** OR **CAPTURED**.

PHILIP IS **PLEASED** WITH ALEXANDER. THE CITY STATES ARE BEATEN AND FORCED TO JOIN THE **LEAGUE OF CORINTH**, WHICH PHILIP LEADS. AT HOME, THINGS ARE **LESS** HAPPY. AS PHILIP'S POWER GROWS, SO DOES HIS LIST OF ENEMIES. ONE NIGHT PHILIP FINDS A **NASTY SURPRISE** IN HIS WIFE'S BED...

HE CANNOT TRUST **ANYONE**...

...EVEN HIS WIFE, OLYMPIAS.

12

IT IS OCTOBER OF THE SAME YEAR AND THE COURT HAS ASSEMBLED FOR THE WEDDING OF PHILIP'S DAUGHTER, CLEOPATRA. AS IS THE CUSTOM, PHILIP MUST WALK ACROSS THE FLOOR OF THE HALL TO GREET THE WEDDING GUESTS. HE IS ALONE AND UNARMED. SUDDENLY...

PAUSANIUS! GET BACK TO YOUR POST! WHAT THE – ?

AHH!

LATER...

YOUR LIFE IS ALSO IN DANGER, ALEXANDER.

YES, MY FATHER'S MURDERERS WILL TRY TO TAKE MY THRONE. BUT WE DO HAVE ALLIES, MOTHER.

I HAVE THE SUPPORT OF GENERALS PARMENION AND ANTIPATER, AND THROUGH THEM, THE ARMY. WITH THEIR HELP, THE DANGER – AND MY ENEMIES – WILL SOON BE GONE.

ALEXANDER'S RIVALS ARE DEALT WITH!

NEWS OF PHILIP'S DEATH *SPREADS QUICKLY.* IN 335 B.C., A REBELLION BREAKS OUT IN THE NORTH. ALEXANDER AND HIS ARMY ARE SOON ON THE MARCH.

THE UPRISING IS PUT DOWN WITH LIGHTNING SPEED. BUT THERE ARE *NEW WORRIES* FOR THE YOUNG KING.

THE CITY STATES, ARE IN **REVOLT**, SIRE!

IN ATHENS, THE RUMORS FLY.

PEOPLE OF ATHENS! NOW IS THE TIME TO RID OURSELVES OF THESE **MACEDONIAN BARBARIANS**! THEBES HAS **ALREADY** RISEN AGAINST THEM! LET **US** FOLLOW ITS EXAMPLE!

HAVE YOU HEARD? THE BOY-KING IS **DEAD**! HE DIED OF HIS WOUNDS!

...MURDERED!

...THE PLAGUE!

...SUICIDE!

IN THE AUTUMN, THEBES IS THE FIRST TO FEEL **ALEXANDER'S FURY**. SURVIVORS ARE SOLD INTO SLAVERY. ATHENS HAS A CHANGE OF HEART.

A MEETING OF THE LEAGUE OF CORINTH.

BEFORE HE WAS MURDERED, MY FATHER PLANNED TO **FREE THE GREEK COLONIES** UNDER **PERSIAN RULE**. WE CAN ONLY DO THIS IF WE ARE **UNITED**.

WE SHALL UNDO **YEARS** OF SHAME AND **CROSS INTO ASIA**!

AND PERHAPS TAKE **PERSIA**?

14

MAY 334 B.C. GREEK SHIPS CARRY ALEXANDER'S ARMY OVER THE **HELLESPONT**, THE WATERS THAT SEPARATE EUROPE AND ASIA.

ALEXANDER IS IN THE LEADING SHIP. AS IT NEARS LAND, ALEXANDER **HURLS** A JAVELIN TOWARD THE SHORE.

THIS LAND IS MINE!

THE PERSIANS MEET TO CREATE A PLAN...

AS LOCAL GOVERNORS, IT IS OUR DUTY TO **DEFEND** THE EMPIRE AGAINST THIS **INVASION**.

GENERAL MEMNON, YOUR THOUGHTS, PLEASE.

I KNEW PHILIP AND I'VE MET THE BOY. HE IS DARING, BRAVE, RECKLESS, AND INTELLIGENT. **DO NOT BE FOOLED** BY HIS YOUTH. HE WILL **NOT** BE AN EASY ENEMY TO BEAT. BUT I HAVE A **PLAN**.

WE WILL **PULL BACK** OUR FORCES AND DRAW HIM INTO THE COUNTRYSIDE. THEN WE'LL **BURN** ALL THE CROPS AND **POISON** EVERY WELL. WHEN HE AND HIS MEN ARE WEAK FROM HUNGER AND THIRST, **THEN WE WILL STRIKE!**

NO! WE CANNOT **RUIN** THE EMPIRE JUST TO DEFEAT THIS BOY! WE SHALL FACE HIM **HERE**, BY THE GRANICUS RIVER. ITS BANKS ARE STEEP, MUDDY, AND SLIPPERY.

WHILE HIS ARMY **FLOUNDERS**, WE SHALL TURN THE WATERS RED WITH *BARBARIAN BLOOD!*

CLITUS!* WELL TIMED, MY FRIEND!

SHUMPHHH!

*CLITUS WAS A COMMANDER WHO HAD FOUGHT UNDER PHILIP.

THE PERSIANS RUN, ALEXANDER. THE BATTLE IS WON.

THE QUESTION IS, CLITUS, WHICH WAY DO WE TURN NOW?

A COUNCIL OF WAR...

WHICH ROAD SHOULD WE TAKE? WE COULD TURN EAST AND FORCE DARIUS TO FIGHT, FACE TO FACE. BUT THERE IS A PROBLEM. GENERAL PARMENION, EXPLAIN.

WE GAVE OUR WORD TO THE LEAGUE. WE WILL GO TO THE COAST AND FREE THE COLONIES.

THE PERSIAN NAVY IS TOO STRONG. IT CAN CONTROL THE COASTLINE, CUTTING US OFF FROM SUPPLIES AND FRESH TROOPS. IT COULD EVEN ATTACK OUR HOMELAND. NO, THIS THREAT MUST BE DEALT WITH BEFORE WE CAN GO EAST.

17

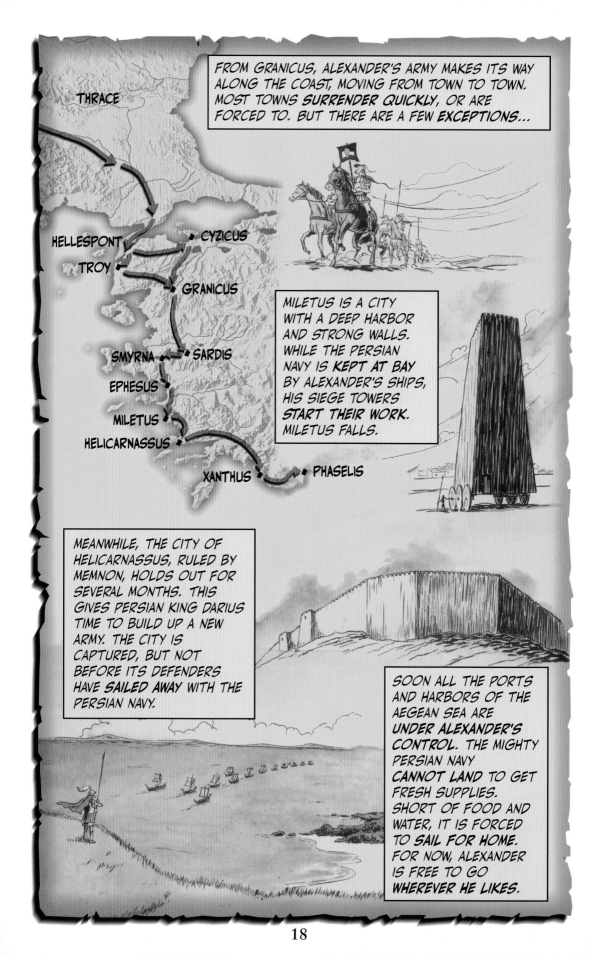

FROM GRANICUS, ALEXANDER'S ARMY MAKES ITS WAY ALONG THE COAST, MOVING FROM TOWN TO TOWN. MOST TOWNS *SURRENDER QUICKLY,* OR ARE FORCED TO. BUT THERE ARE A FEW *EXCEPTIONS...*

THRACE

HELLESPONT

TROY

CYZICUS

GRANICUS

SMYRNA — SARDIS

EPHESUS

MILETUS

HELICARNASSUS

XANTHUS • PHASELIS

MILETUS IS A CITY WITH A DEEP HARBOR AND STRONG WALLS. WHILE THE PERSIAN NAVY IS *KEPT AT BAY* BY ALEXANDER'S SHIPS, HIS SIEGE TOWERS *START THEIR WORK.* MILETUS FALLS.

MEANWHILE, THE CITY OF HELICARNASSUS, RULED BY MEMNON, HOLDS OUT FOR SEVERAL MONTHS. THIS GIVES PERSIAN KING DARIUS TIME TO BUILD UP A NEW ARMY. THE CITY IS CAPTURED, BUT NOT BEFORE ITS DEFENDERS HAVE *SAILED AWAY* WITH THE PERSIAN NAVY.

SOON ALL THE PORTS AND HARBORS OF THE AEGEAN SEA ARE *UNDER ALEXANDER'S CONTROL.* THE MIGHTY PERSIAN NAVY *CANNOT LAND* TO GET FRESH SUPPLIES. SHORT OF FOOD AND WATER, IT IS FORCED TO *SAIL FOR HOME.* FOR NOW, ALEXANDER IS FREE TO GO *WHEREVER HE LIKES.*

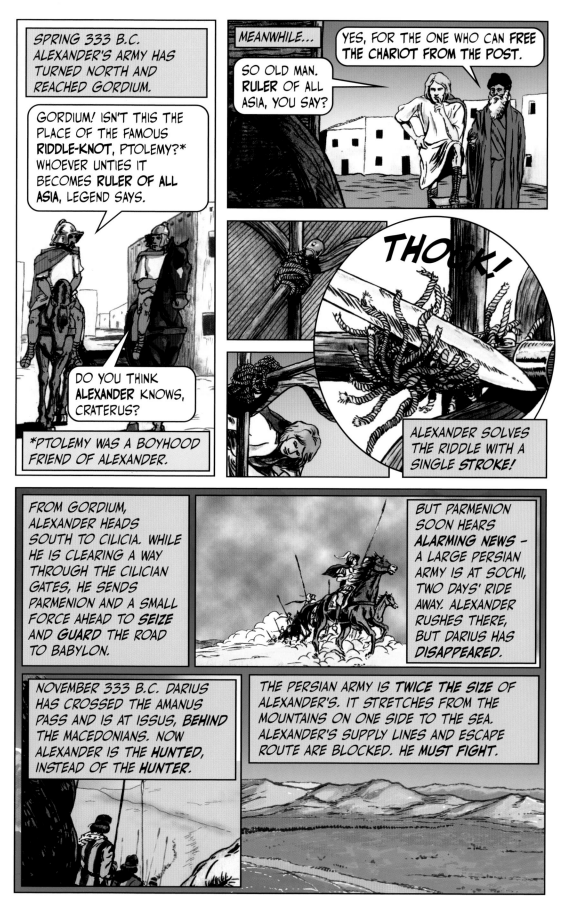

SPRING 333 B.C. ALEXANDER'S ARMY HAS TURNED NORTH AND REACHED GORDIUM.

GORDIUM! ISN'T THIS THE PLACE OF THE FAMOUS **RIDDLE-KNOT**, PTOLEMY?* WHOEVER UNTIES IT BECOMES **RULER OF ALL ASIA**, LEGEND SAYS.

DO YOU THINK **ALEXANDER** KNOWS, CRATERUS?

*PTOLEMY WAS A BOYHOOD FRIEND OF ALEXANDER.

MEANWHILE...

SO OLD MAN. **RULER** OF ALL ASIA, YOU SAY?

YES, FOR THE ONE WHO CAN **FREE** THE CHARIOT FROM THE POST.

THOCK!

ALEXANDER SOLVES THE RIDDLE WITH A SINGLE **STROKE!**

FROM GORDIUM, ALEXANDER HEADS SOUTH TO CILICIA. WHILE HE IS CLEARING A WAY THROUGH THE CILICIAN GATES, HE SENDS PARMENION AND A SMALL FORCE AHEAD TO **SEIZE** AND **GUARD** THE ROAD TO BABYLON.

BUT PARMENION SOON HEARS **ALARMING NEWS** – A LARGE PERSIAN ARMY IS AT SOCHI, TWO DAYS' RIDE AWAY. ALEXANDER RUSHES THERE, BUT DARIUS HAS **DISAPPEARED.**

NOVEMBER 333 B.C. DARIUS HAS CROSSED THE AMANUS PASS AND IS AT ISSUS, **BEHIND** THE MACEDONIANS. NOW ALEXANDER IS THE **HUNTED**, INSTEAD OF THE **HUNTER.**

THE PERSIAN ARMY IS **TWICE THE SIZE** OF ALEXANDER'S. IT STRETCHES FROM THE MOUNTAINS ON ONE SIDE TO THE SEA. ALEXANDER'S SUPPLY LINES AND ESCAPE ROUTE ARE BLOCKED. HE **MUST FIGHT.**

AS USUAL, ALEXANDER'S CAVALRY *MOVES FORWARD* AND TO THE RIGHT. IT WAITS FOR A GAP TO APPEAR IN THE PERSIAN LINE.

WATCHING FROM HIS CHARIOT, DARIUS REALIZES HE HAS *MADE A MISTAKE.* THE GROUND IS *TOO ROCKY* TO USE HIS *CHARIOTS.* THE PERSIANS FOLLOW ALEXANDER'S CAVALRY, THINNING THEIR LINE. A GAP *APPEARS* AND ALEXANDER *CHARGES.*

THE MACEDONIANS *CUT THROUGH* THE PERSIANS, *SCATTERING* THEM. HIS BODYGUARD IS KILLED AND *DARIUS FLEES.* THE BATTLE IS WON IN UNDER AN HOUR. LATER, ALEXANDER HAS A SPECIAL MISSION FOR PARMENION IN DAMASCUS.

IN DAMASCUS, THE LOCAL RULER AND THE GUARDIAN OF THE PERSIANS' WESTERN TREASURY IS ENJOYING HIS SUPPER.

AH, I HEAR RIDERS. THIS IS NEWS OF A *VICTORY,* I AM SURE.

MY LORD! THE MACEDONIANS! *THEY'RE HERE!*

BACK AT THE MACEDONIAN CAMP...

WELL DONE, PARMENION! THE WHOLE TREASURY IS *OURS!*

THEY HADN'T HEARD THE NEWS FROM ISSUS SO THE *GOLD* WAS STILL *THERE.* WE FOUND *SOMETHING ELSE* BELONGING TO DARIUS — HIS WIFE, HIS CHILDREN, AND...HIS *MOTHER.*

COME, HEPHAESTION. LET US *GREET* THE MOTHER OF A KING!

A SLIGHT CONFUSION!

MIGHTY ALEXANDER!

MADAM, I AM ALEXANDER! FROM NOW ON, *YOU AND YOUR FAMILY* ARE GUESTS AND UNDER MY *PROTECTION.*

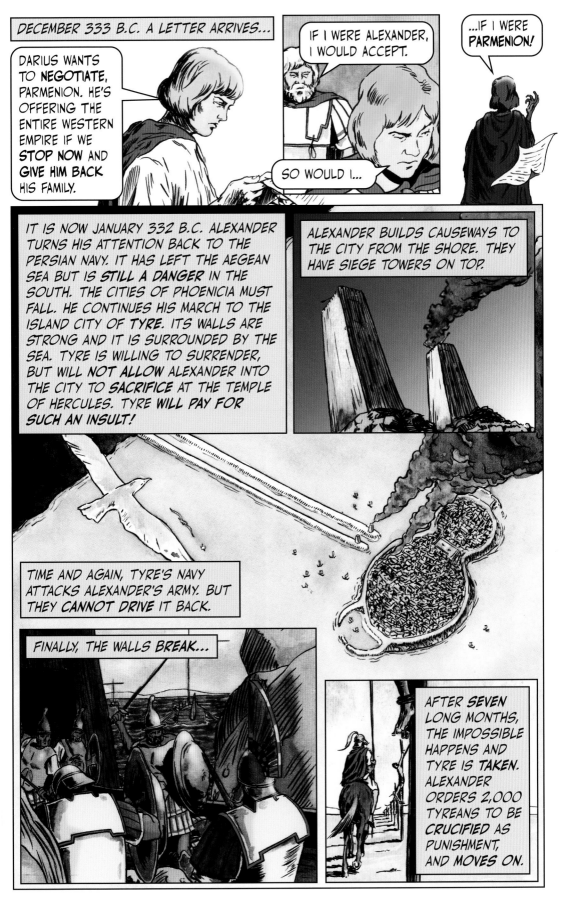

DECEMBER 333 B.C. A LETTER ARRIVES...

DARIUS WANTS TO **NEGOTIATE**, PARMENION. HE'S OFFERING THE ENTIRE WESTERN EMPIRE IF WE **STOP NOW** AND **GIVE HIM BACK** HIS FAMILY.

IF I WERE ALEXANDER, I WOULD ACCEPT.

...IF I WERE **PARMENION!**

SO WOULD I...

IT IS NOW JANUARY 332 B.C. ALEXANDER TURNS HIS ATTENTION BACK TO THE PERSIAN NAVY. IT HAS LEFT THE AEGEAN SEA BUT IS **STILL A DANGER** IN THE SOUTH. THE CITIES OF PHOENICIA MUST FALL. HE CONTINUES HIS MARCH TO THE ISLAND CITY OF **TYRE**. ITS WALLS ARE STRONG AND IT IS SURROUNDED BY THE SEA. TYRE IS WILLING TO SURRENDER, BUT WILL **NOT ALLOW** ALEXANDER INTO THE CITY TO **SACRIFICE** AT THE TEMPLE OF HERCULES. TYRE **WILL PAY FOR SUCH AN INSULT!**

ALEXANDER BUILDS CAUSEWAYS TO THE CITY FROM THE SHORE. THEY HAVE SIEGE TOWERS ON TOP.

TIME AND AGAIN, TYRE'S NAVY ATTACKS ALEXANDER'S ARMY. BUT THEY **CANNOT DRIVE** IT BACK.

FINALLY, THE WALLS BREAK...

AFTER **SEVEN** LONG MONTHS, THE IMPOSSIBLE HAPPENS AND TYRE IS **TAKEN**. ALEXANDER ORDERS 2,000 TYREANS TO BE **CRUCIFIED** AS PUNISHMENT, AND **MOVES ON**.

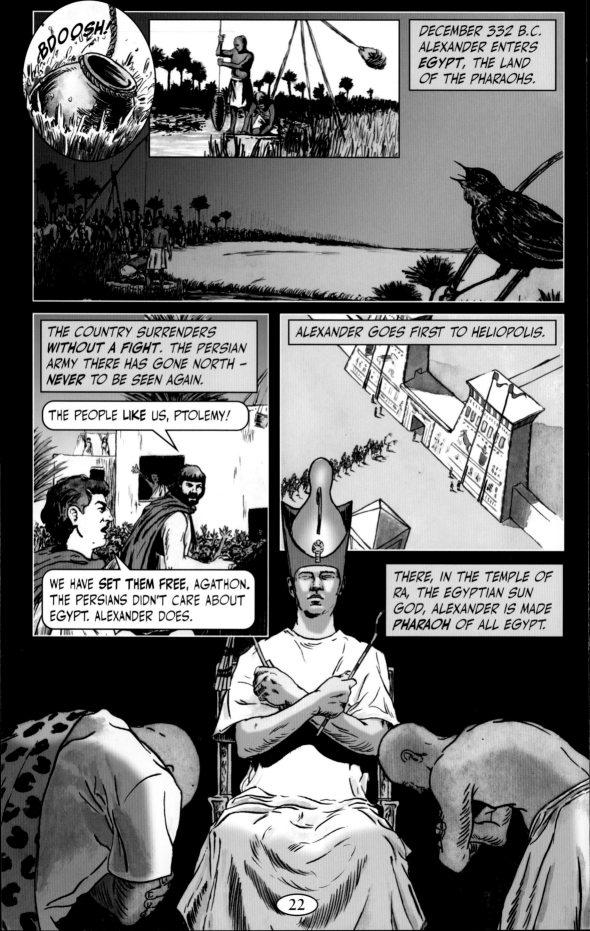

BDOOSH!

DECEMBER 332 B.C. ALEXANDER ENTERS *EGYPT*, THE LAND OF THE PHARAOHS.

THE COUNTRY SURRENDERS *WITHOUT A FIGHT.* THE PERSIAN ARMY THERE HAS GONE NORTH — *NEVER TO BE SEEN AGAIN.*

THE PEOPLE *LIKE* US, PTOLEMY!

WE HAVE *SET THEM FREE,* AGATHON. THE PERSIANS DIDN'T CARE ABOUT EGYPT. ALEXANDER DOES.

ALEXANDER GOES FIRST TO HELIOPOLIS.

THERE, IN THE TEMPLE OF RA, THE EGYPTIAN SUN GOD, ALEXANDER IS MADE *PHARAOH* OF ALL EGYPT.

THE NEW PHARAOH LEAVES HELIOPOLIS. HE VISITS THE CITY OF **MEMPHIS** AND THEN TRAVELS TO SEE THE **GREAT PYRAMIDS OF GIZA**, OLD EVEN IN ALEXANDER'S DAY.

THE GROUP FOLLOWS THE **NILE RIVER** TO ITS DELTA AT THE COAST. ALEXANDER HAS A **PLAN**.

I WILL BUILD A NEW CITY AND CALL IT **ALEXANDRIA**. THE OLD GREEK TRADING PORT IS TOO FAR INLAND. A CITY HERE WOULD BE OPEN TO THE SEA AND THE NILE RIVER. GREECE WILL BE ABLE TO **TRADE** ITS GOODS FOR EGYPTIAN GRAIN.

I WANT THE CITY TO BECOME A CENTER FOR **LEARNING AND CULTURE**, A PLACE WHERE THE FINEST MINDS IN THE WORLD WILL GATHER.

WHERE TO **NOW**, ALEXANDER?

HERCULES ONCE CAME TO EGYPT AND MADE A **JOURNEY** INTO THE DESERT. WE WILL MAKE THAT SAME JOURNEY. THERE'S **SOMEONE** I WOULD **LIKE TO MEET** OUT THERE.

THE DESERT TREK IS A DIFFICULT ONE.	THEY MARCH THROUGH SANDSTORMS...	...AND RAINSTORMS.

AFTER MANY DAYS, THEY REACH THEIR DESTINATION, THE OASIS CITY OF SIWA.

ALEXANDER GOES TO THE TEMPLE TO SEE THE ORACLE. THIS IS THE REASON FOR HIS JOURNEY. HE IS TOLD WHAT HE WANTS TO KNOW.*

*ALEXANDER WILL ONLY REVEAL WHAT HE HAS BEEN TOLD TO HIS MOTHER, SO NO ONE KNOWS EXACTLY WHAT WAS SAID.

HE LEAVES THE TEMPLE AS ALEXANDER, SON OF THE GOD AMMON!

THE TIME SPENT IN EGYPT HAS BEEN PLEASANT. REFRESHED, ALEXANDER IS READY TO LEAVE. IN THE SUMMER OF 331 B.C., THE ARMY TURNS NORTH AND MARCHES OUT OF EGYPT FOR ONE LAST BATTLE WITH DARIUS.

ALEXANDER AND HIS ARMY HEAD **NORTH**, HUNTING FOR DARIUS. A SMALL PERSIAN FORCE **FOLLOWS** BEHIND...

DO WE **ATTACK THEM?**

NO. A FIGHT MAY WEAKEN US. WE NEED TO BE **STRONG** TO FACE DARIUS.

THEY CROSS THE TIGRIS RIVER. IT IS ONLY LIGHTLY DEFENDED. ALEXANDER DOES NOT KNOW IT YET BUT HE HAS **ENTERED A TRAP!**

DARIUS IS TOLD OF ALEXANDER'S **PROGRESS**...

HE TOOK THE BAIT, MY LORD, AND IS MARCHING TO **GAUGAMELA**, AND OUR **ARMY**.

OUR SIDES WILL BE PROTECTED BY SPIKES AND THE GROUND LEVELED INTO RUNWAYS FOR THE CHARIOTS. I WILL **BREAK HIM** AND HIS ARMY. HE SHALL **NOT ESCAPE** ME THIS TIME!

EXCELLENT NEWS, **MAZAEUS!**

YOU HAVE HERDED THEM BEFORE YOU LIKE SHEEP TO MARKET. ONCE AGAIN I HAVE OUTFOXED HIM! BUT I WILL BE **MORE CAREFUL** THAN AT ISSUS.

SEPTEMBER 331 B.C. AT GAUGAMELA, "THE CAMEL'S BACK," ALEXANDER FINDS DARIUS. THAT EVENING, HE GAZES UPON THE MANY FIRES OF THE HUGE PERSIAN ARMY.

WE SHOULD STRIKE **NOW**, ALEXANDER!

PTOLEMY, WE FACE AN ARMY FIVE TIMES LARGER THAN OUR OWN. YET ALEXANDER PLANS TO KEEP SOME MEN IN **RESERVE!**

I DO NOT **STEAL** MY VICTORIES, PARMENION!

HE MUST HAVE HIS REASONS, CRATERUS.

THE NEXT MORNING, OCTOBER 1, THE PERSIANS ARE **READY.**

ALEXANDER IS RIGHT **NOT** TO ATTACK DURING THE NIGHT. DARIUS HAS KEPT HIS WHOLE ARMY AWAKE FOR SUCH AN EVENT. IN THE MORNING, THE AIR IS FILLED WITH THE SOUND OF MANY DIFFERENT LANGUAGES FROM ALL OVER THE EMPIRE. TO THE REAR ARE A SLEEPY TROOP OF EASTERN TRIBESMEN.

WAKE UP! CAN ANYONE **SEE** ANYTHING? IS THERE **MOVEMENT** OUT THERE?

WHAA?

25

THE MACEDONIANS START *MOVING TOWARD* THE PERSIAN TROOPS. THEY DO NOT MARCH IN A STRAIGHT LINE. THEY ARE SLOWLY DRIFTING *TO THEIR RIGHT*, AND AT AN ANGLE. THE RIGHT WING IS CLOSER TO THE PERSIANS THAN THE LEFT.

THE TWO TRIBESMEN ARE HAVING TROUBLE FOLLOWING THE ACTION.

WHAT'S HAPPENING *NOW?* WHERE ARE ALL OUR *COMMANDERS?*

LOOK! THERE'S AN OFFICER. FIND OUT WHAT'S GOING ON.

IT'S NO USE. I DON'T KNOW WHAT HE'S SAYING. HE'S SPEAKING A LANGUAGE I CANNOT UNDERSTAND.

THE TACTIC USED AT ISSUS *WORKS AGAIN.* A WEAKNESS APPEARS IN THE PERSIAN LINES AND ALEXANDER *CHARGES.* HIS CAVALRY *SMASHES* INTO THE PERSIANS. BEHIND THE CAVALRY, THE INFANTRY *MOVES FORWARD* AND ATTACKS.

THE SUDDEN RUSH HAS *CAUSED PROBLEMS* ON THE LEFT. A GAP HAS OPENED IN ALEXANDER'S *OWN LINE.* PARMENION COMES UNDER *HEAVY PRESSURE* AND IS NEARLY SURROUNDED. THE RESERVE TROOPS COME TO HIS *RESCUE* AND THE ATTACKERS ARE *DRIVEN OFF.*

DARIUS ORDERS HIS 200 CHARIOTS TO CHARGE, BUT *IT IS TOO LATE!* THE MACEDONIANS HAVE MOVED AWAY FROM THE RUNWAYS. THE CHARGE IS MET BY A HAIL OF JAVELINS, AND STOPPED. DARIUS KNOWS HE HAS *LOST.*

THE ENEMY SHOULD BE IN **FRONT** OF US! WHERE **ARE** THEY?

WHERE ARE THEY?

ALEXANDER HAS *CARVED* HIS WAY INTO THE PERSIANS AND NOW HE TURNS LEFT. HE HAS ONLY ONE AIM – *TO GET TO DARIUS!* SEEING HIS MEN DYING AROUND HIM, *DARIUS FLEES* – ONCE AGAIN.

WHERE **ARE** THEY? THEY'RE ON TOP OF US! RUN, YOU FOOL! **RUN!**

THE **BATTLE** TURNS INTO A **CHASE** AND THE **CHASE** BECOMES A **SLAUGHTER.** THE MACEDONIANS FOLLOW THE PERSIANS FOR MANY MILES, THEN HEAD BACK TO CAMP. THEIR LOSSES ARE LIGHT. THE PERSIAN LOSSES ARE **ENORMOUS.**

THE ROAD EAST IS *CLEAR*. ON OCTOBER 21, 331 B.C., ALEXANDER PASSES THROUGH THE *ISHTAR GATE* AND *INTO* THE CITY OF BABYLON.

THE FOLLOWING YEAR, HIS ARMY *SWEEPS* THROUGH A MOUNTAIN PASS CALLED THE *PERSIAN GATES*.

THEY REACH *PERSEPOLIS*, CITY OF THE PERSIANS, IN THE SPRING.

ALEXANDER *ENTERS* DARIUS'S PALACE, AND *SITS* ON HIS GOLDEN THRONE.

SO *THIS* IS WHAT IT IS LIKE TO BE A *KING!*

THE ROYAL PALACES ARE *STRIPPED* OF THEIR TREASURES. THE CITY ITSELF IS GIVEN OVER TO THE TROOPS TO ENJOY. MEANWHILE, ALEXANDER IS *WAITING*.

WE HAVE BEEN HERE FOR *FOUR MONTHS* NOW, ALEXANDER. WHY DO WE STAY?

I WANTED TO WAIT UNTIL THE NEW YEAR FESTIVAL, HEPHAESTION. I HOPED THE PERSIAN NOBLES WOULD GIVE ME THEIR *SUPPORT*.

WITHOUT IT, THE PERSIAN PEOPLE WILL *NOT ACCEPT* ME AS THEIR KING.

BUT THEY HAVE NOT COME, AND *WILL NOT* COME WHILE DARIUS IS STILL *ALIVE*.

YET I *CANNOT* KILL DARIUS. THE PERSIANS WOULD *HATE ME*. THEN I COULD *NEVER* BE THEIR TRUE KING.

DARIUS IS TAKEN **PRISONER** AND BUNDLED INTO A CART. WHEN THE MACEDONIAN CAVALRY IS **SPOTTED**, HIS CAPTORS **PANIC**. BY THE TIME THE SOLDIERS ARRIVE, DARIUS IS **DEAD**.

DARIUS'S BODY WILL BE SENT TO PERSEPOLIS FOR A **ROYAL BURIAL**. I NEEDED HIM DEAD BUT COULD **NOT** KILL HIM. THE PERSIANS WOULD NOT HAVE FORGIVEN ME. BESSUS HAS GIVEN ME THE **EXCUSE** TO **CONQUER THE EAST**, PUNISH THIS MURDER, AND WIN THE PERSIANS' **THANKS**.

MEANWHILE, ALEXANDER IS TOLD ABOUT A **PLOT** AGAINST HIM...

WE WOULD HAVE TOLD YOU ABOUT IT **SOONER** BUT WERE STOPPED BY **PHILOTAS**.

PARMENION'S **SON**!

THIS IS **NOT** THE FIRST TIME HE HAS TRIED TO **CHEAT** ME.

I **FORGAVE** MY FRIEND BEFORE. BUT I **CANNOT** HELP HIM **NOW**.

PARMENION IS IN ECBATANA. HE COULD BE **DANGEROUS**.

A MESSAGE IS SENT TO ECBATANA'S COMMANDER. GENERAL PARMENION NEVER HEARS OF HIS SON'S EXECUTION – THE OLD MAN IS ASSASSINATED.

THE **HUNT** IS NOW ON FOR **BESSUS**. HE WILL NOT BE EXPECTING THE MACEDONIANS TO REACH BACTRIA BY CROSSING THE **HINDU KUSH MOUNTAINS** IN THE THICK OF **WINTER**.

THE PLAN **WORKS**. BEFORE LONG, PTOLEMY BRINGS ALEXANDER A **GIFT**.

BESSUS! THE KING KILLER. SEND HIM TO DARIUS'S BROTHER. HE HAS MORE **REASON** TO JUDGE BESSUS THAN I.

THE SOGDIANS THINK THEMSELVES **SAFE** UP ON THEIR HIGH ROCK. THE SLOPES ARE HEAVILY DEFENDED. BUT TO THE REAR, THE WALLS OF THE CLIFF ARE TOO STEEP TO CLIMB AND SO ARE **NOT WATCHED.** TONIGHT YOU WILL **CLIMB** THAT CLIFF. WHEN THEY SEE YOU AT THEIR BACKS, THEY WILL NOT FIGHT. SOME OF YOU WILL **NOT REACH** THE TOP. BUT THERE WILL BE **GOLD** FOR THE **FIRST** MEN UP!

AIIEEEE!

THINKING THAT ALL OF ALEXANDER'S ARMY HAS BEEN "GIVEN WINGS," THE SOGDIANS MEEKLY SURRENDER.

OF THE 300 THAT STOOD AT THE FOOT OF THE CLIFF, 30 DO NOT LIVE TO STAND ON ITS PEAK.

LATE WINTER 326 B.C. THE ARMY MOVES SOUTH...

I UNDERSTOOD THE NEED TO CONQUER BACTRIA. BUT WHY HEAD **SOUTH**?

CURIOSITY, MAYBE? OR **GOLD**? THERE'S PLENTY OVER THE INDUS RIVER.

SO, NOW WE ARE EXPLORERS, OR **COMMON THIEVES**?

I WOULDN'T LET **ALEXANDER** HEAR YOU SAY THAT!

TO REACH INDIA, ALEXANDER MUST CROSS KING PORUS'S LANDS. AT THE RIVER HYDASPES, THEY MEET PORUS'S ARMY. IT IS SMALL BUT THE KING HAS A **POWERFUL** WEAPON. LINED UP IN FRONT OF HIS MEN IS A TERRIFYING, **TOWERING GRAY WALL** OF **200 ELEPHANTS!** THE MACEDONIANS HAVE SEEN ELEPHANTS BEFORE, BUT NOT THIS MANY.

THE TWO ARMIES WATCH EACH OTHER CAREFULLY FOR MANY DAYS. AT NIGHT, ALEXANDER MOVES HIS ARMY ACROSS THE RIVER. PORUS IS CAUGHT BY **SURPRISE**.

ALEXANDER DARE NOT ATTACK FROM THE FRONT. HE MANAGES TO GET BEHIND PORUS. THE INDIAN CHARIOTS ARE DRIVEN AMONG THE ELEPHANTS, CAUSING **PANIC**. JAVELINS AND ARROWS **RAIN DOWN** ON THE BEASTS. **MADDENED** BY THEIR WOUNDS, INJURED ELEPHANTS **STAMPEDE** THROUGH THE TROOPS, **TRAMPLING** BOTH MACEDONIANS AND INDIANS.

PORUS **SURRENDERS**. HIS ARMY IS **WIPED OUT**. ALEXANDER IS KIND AND ALLOWS PORUS TO RULE HIS OWN KINGDOM. THE MACEDONIANS HAVE **SUFFERED BADLY**. THEY ARE NEVER THE SAME FORCE **AGAIN**.

SPLOOSH!

IN THE SUMMER, THE ARMY PUSHES DEEPER INTO INDIA.

DID YOU EVER SEE SUCH RAIN!

THE LOCALS CALL IT A MONSOON.

IT'S THE SAME, DAY AFTER DAY, AT EXACTLY THE SAME TIME!

WHAT ARE WE DOING HERE? HAVEN'T WE BEATEN THE PERSIANS?

WORD IS, WE CROSS THE HYPHASIS RIVER TOMORROW. IT'S TWICE AS WIDE AS THE NILE AND AS DEEP AS A PYRAMID! AND THERE ARE CROCODILES.

I CAN'T SEE US EVER GETTING HOME.

AND WHAT'S ON THE OTHER SIDE, EH? THOUSANDS OF UNFRIENDLY LOCALS, WHO WON'T WANT US THERE.

THE ORDER IS GIVEN TO MOVE. NOTHING HAPPENS. THE MEN REFUSE TO GO ANY FARTHER EASTWARD.

COME ON! UP! SHIFT YOURSELVES! WHAT'S WRONG WITH YOU ALL?

ALEXANDER IS TOLD.

MUTINY, SIRE!

ALEXANDER GOES TO HIS TENT...

...TO BROOD, SILENTLY.

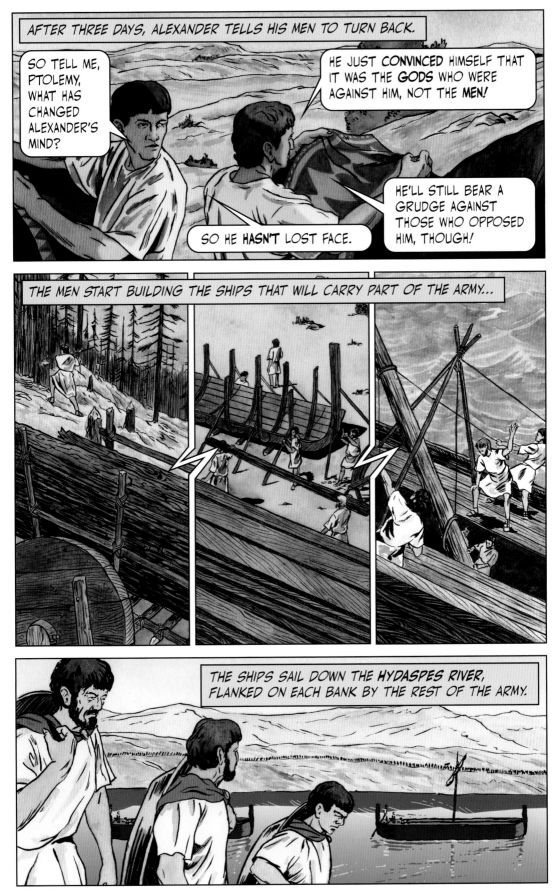

JANUARY 325 B.C. THE MARCH DOWN THE RIVER IS NOT EASY. EVERY CITY, TOWN, AND VILLAGE SEEMS TO WANT TO FIGHT. AT THE CITY OF A TRIBE CALLED THE MALLI, ALEXANDER IS THE FIRST OVER THE WALLS.

ALMOST AS SOON AS HE IS IN THE CITY, ALEXANDER IS **HIT** BY **AN ARROW.**

HE IS SAVED BY **ACHILLES'** **SACRED SHIELD.**

ALEXANDER **RECOVERS** AND THE NAVY CARRIES ON. BUT THERE ARE RISKS AHEAD. WHERE THE RIVER MEETS THE INDUS RIVER, THE CURRENTS CAN BE **DANGEROUS** FOR CARELESS CAPTAINS...

MANY SHIPS AND LIVES ARE LOST.

THE REMAINING SHIPS SAIL ON TO THE COAST. THERE THEY ARE REPAIRED AND FILLED WITH FRESH SUPPLIES OVER THE SPRING. ALEXANDER AND HIS ADMIRAL, NEARCHUS, INSPECT THE WORK.

HOW LONG BEFORE THE SHIPS ARE READY, NEARCHUS?

THREE MONTHS AT THE EARLIEST.

THE ARMY WILL MOVE OUT FIRST AND MAKE ITS WAY ALONG THE COAST.

WHEN THE SHIPS ARE **READY**, BRING THE SUPPLIES. WE WILL MEET YOU AT **GWADAR**.

THE ARMY LEAVES THE NAVY BEHIND.

LIKE LOCUSTS, THE ARMY STRIPS THE LAND **BARE** OF FOOD. AS ALWAYS, IT IS THE LOCAL POPULATION THAT **SUFFERS MOST**.

NEARCHUS, THE NAVY, AND SUPPLIES HAVE NOT YET ARRIVED AS PLANNED.

THE SITUATION IS **NOT GOOD**. WE CANNOT GO FORWARD **OR** BACK. THERE IS **NO** FOOD. THE SHIPS MAY HAVE **SUNK** FOR ALL WE KNOW. THE ONLY THING WE CAN DO IS TO GO INLAND TO PURA, THROUGH THE GEDROSIAN DESERT.

IT WILL BE **DIFFICULT**. CYRUS THE GREAT ONCE LOST A WHOLE ARMY THERE. BUT WE WILL BE GOING DURING THE WET SEASON. THERE WILL BE FODDER AND THE WELLS WILL BE FULL. IF THE GODS ARE KIND, WE WILL REACH SAFETY.

I THOUGHT THIS WAS THE **RAINY** SEASON!

BUT THE RAINS ARE **LATE** THIS YEAR.

THEN COME THE STORMS...

FLASH FLOOD!

IT IS HARD GOING FOR THE ARMY AND EVEN HARDER FOR THE ANIMALS, WOMEN, AND CHILDREN TRAVELING ALONG WITH IT.

OCTOBER 325 B.C. AFTER 60 DAYS, THEY REACH PURA. THOUSANDS HAVE *DIED* ON THE MURDEROUS MARCH.

THE ORDEAL IS OVER. TO *CELEBRATE*, ALEXANDER THROWS A PARTY!

YOU LOOK WORRIED, ALEXANDER.

IT'S THE ARMY. SOME MEN HAVE BEEN WITH ME FROM THE START. THEY'RE GETTING *OLD*. THERE WILL HAVE TO BE CHANGES.

THE FOLLOWING YEAR AT OPIS, THE MEN ARE TO BE REPLACED BY 30,000 *PERSIAN YOUTHS* AND SENT HOME, WELL REWARDED. THE ARMY IS *NOT HAPPY*, THOUGH. THEY THINK ALEXANDER IS BECOMING *TOO PERSIAN*, WITH HIS PERSIAN FRIENDS AND CLOTHING. THEY *DO NOT LIKE* THE CHANGES, AND THEY *SAY SO*!

GO FIGHT YOUR WARS WITH YOUR FATHER AMMON!

AND YOUR NEW PERSIAN FRIENDS!

LOOK AT HIM! HE LETS THE PERSIANS GREET HIM AS IF HE WAS ONE OF THEM! HE'S *MORE PERSIAN* THAN MACEDONIAN!

WE MACEDONIANS MEAN *NOTHING* TO YOU. ALL YOU WANT IS TO BE *ANOTHER* PERSIAN TYRANT!

UNGRATEFUL MACEDONIANS! YOU WERE ONCE THE *SLAVES* OF THE PERSIANS. I HAVE MADE YOU THEIR *MASTERS*. I HAVE MADE YOU ALL *RICH*.

I *DISMISS* YOU ALL! AND YOU LEAVE WITH *NOTHING*!

ALEXANDER GOES TO HIS TENT, AS HE DID AT THE HYPHASIS.

THE ARMY IS ASHAMED OF ITS BEHAVIOR. THE MEN STAND OUTSIDE HIS TENT AND *REFUSE* TO LEAVE UNTIL THEY ARE *FORGIVEN*. AFTER TWO DAYS AND NIGHTS, ALEXANDER *SOFTENS*. THE MEN WILL STILL GO HOME BUT WITH THE PROMISED REWARDS.

HAVING GOT HIS WAY, ALEXANDER GOES TO ECBATANA.

41

AFTER ALEXANDER

When Alexander died in Babylon in 323 B.C., he left no plans for how his empire should be governed. Alexander's generals fought over the empire and finally divided it among themselves.

WESTERN
EMPIRE
Antigonas

EASTERN
EMPIRE
Seleucus

EGYPT
Ptolemy

This map shows how Alexander's huge empire was divided among the families of three of his generals – Antigonas, Ptolemy, and Seleucus.

POWER STRUGGLE

After Alexander's death, his baby son and half-brother were both crowned king. But the real power lay in the hands of his generals, the Diadochi. In the struggle for control, Alexander's mother, wife, son, sister, and half-brother were all murdered. Then the empire was split among the Diadochi.

A DIVIDED EMPIRE

By 281 B.C., the War of the Diadochi ended and three rival kingdoms were set up. These were ruled by the families of three of Alexander's generals – Antigonas, Ptolemy, and Seleucus. Antigonas's family seized power in Macedonia and Greece. Ptolemy's family ruled Egypt until 30 B.C. Seleucus's family seized huge areas of Persia but found it hard to control all their lands. By the first century B.C., however, all three kingdoms had been conquered by the Romans.

Alexander's conquests spread Greek culture across large parts of the world. This continued for about 300 years after his death.

ALEXANDER'S LEGACY

As Alexander's empire spread, so did Greek culture and ideas. After Alexander's death, these ideas continued to influence the places he had conquered. In northwest India, for example, art and sculpture showed a mixture of Indian and Greek styles. Alexander built many new cities on his travels. Under Ptolemy, Alexandria became the capital of Egypt. As Alexander had wished, it became an important center of trade and learning. The Greek world's greatest scientists and inventors traveled there to study in the museum's library.

ALEXANDER TODAY

Alexander died over 2,300 years ago. Yet his amazing story still inspires people today. It has been retold many times in books, films, and TV programs. Alexander is remembered as a great hero and leader. His extraordinary courage won great loyalty from his friends and troops who were willing to follow him almost anywhere.

A great marble lighthouse, the Pharos, was built in the harbor at Alexandria. Standing about 590 feet tall (180 meters), it was one of the Seven Wonders of the Ancient World.

45

GLOSSARY

Achilles' sacred shield The shield used by Achilles in the Siege of Troy.

allies People that give support to one another.

assassinate To murder someone who is well known.

captor Someone who takes another person as a prisoner.

causeways Raised roads built across water.

cavalry Soldiers who fight on horseback.

Cilician Gates A mountain pass in Cilicia, near Isis.

city states Independent areas in Ancient Greece.

colonies Territories that are settled by people from another country.

crucified When someone is nailed to a cross to die.

descended Belonging to a later generation of the same family.

execution The killing of someone as punishment for a crime.

flounder To struggle with something.

fodder Food for cattle and horses.

Iliad A poem by the Greek poet, Homer, telling the story of the Trojan War.

infantry The part of an army that fights on foot.

javelin A light spear thrown as a weapon in battle.

League of Corinth A group of all the Greek city states, led by Philip II.

legacy Something passed on to those who come at a later time.

monsoon Strong winds that often bring on heavy rains.

mutiny A revolt against someone in charge.

oasis A place in the desert where there is water, and trees and plants grow.

omens Signs which warn of good or evil to come.

oracle A place where people went to ask the gods for advice.

ordeal A difficult or painful experience.

pauper A very poor person who receives money from others.

phalanx A group of soldiers who fight together.

rebellion Any struggle against the people in charge of something.

revolt To fight against authority.

rumor Something said by people that may not be true.

siege The surrounding of a place to force its people to surrender.

siege towers Towers used in a siege to let soldiers climb an enemy wall.

slaughter The brutal killing of a large number of people.

squabble A noisy argument, usually over something unimportant.

stampede A sudden, wild rush in one direction.

superstitious To believe that an action not connected to a future event can influence the outcome of the event.

trek A slow difficult journey, usually made on foot.

tyrant Someone who rules in a cruel or unfair way.

FOR MORE INFORMATION

ORGANIZATIONS

Kelsey Museum of Archaeology
University of Michigan
434 South State Street
Ann Arbor, MI 48109
(734) 764-9304
Web site: http://www.lsa.umich.edu/kelsey/

University of Pennsylvania Museum of Archaeology and Anthropology
3260 South Street
Philadelphia, PA 19104
(215) 898-4000
Web Site: http://www.museum.upenn.edu

FOR FURTHER READING

Coolidge, Olivia E. *The Trojan War.* Boston, MA: Houghton Mifflin Company, 2001.

Greenblatt, Miriam. *Alexander the Great and Ancient Greece.* Tarrytown, NY: Marshall Cavendish, 1999.

Malam, John. *Exploring Ancient Greece.* London, England: Evans Brothers, Ltd., 1999.

Nardo, Don. *Leaders of Ancient Greece.* Farmington Hills: MI: Gale Group, 1999.

Wepman, Dennis. *Alexander the Great.* Broomall, PA: Chelsea House Publishers, 1986.

INDEX

Web Sites

Due to the changing nature of Internet links, the Rosen Publishing Group, Inc., has developed an online list of Web sites related to the subject of this book. This site is updated regularly. Please use this link to access the list:

http://www.rosenlinks.com/gnf/alex